How To Get Rid of Your Mortgage

Lose Your Mortgage
Own Your Home

2nd Edition

by Patricia Crowe
Edited by Laura Wertz

Richer Resources Press
Arlington, VA

How to Get Rid of Your Mortgage
Lose Your Mortgage
own Your Home

Inquiries and requests for additional copies of this publication should
be addressed to:
Richer Resources Press
P. O. Box 7411
Arlington, VA 22207
or via our web site
www.RicherResourcesPress.com

ISBN 978-0-9776269-2-2
Library of Congress Control Number:
2006901832

TABLE OF CONTENTS

Introduction

This book is intended to bring you, the home buyer, closer to an understanding of the facts of the Mortgage Game, so that you can be more in control of your own home mortgage.

Although the U.S. Truth in Lending Law requires that a lender disclose to a borrower the truth about their loan - what their interest rate will be, how much they will pay in interest on the loan they are getting over the term of the loan, and the total amount they will repay on that loan, many people, when getting their loan, yet do not fully understand certain things about their loans. Such as, why is that the amount they are required to repay, how can they, within the terms of their loan and their knowledge of loan workings, repay this loan faster and less expensively.

The fixed rate compounded interest loan, amortized over 30 or 40 years is a banking innovation pretty much limited to the confines of this country and it makes for a very expensive loan, as you will see within the pages of this book.

Furthermore, as is the case with many professionals in this day, the theory behind how this banking or lending system works is a body of data which is made to seem complex to the average home buyer by virtue of the fact that no one has taken the initiative to explain it to them. It's not even that it would be difficult to explain; it's just that few professional individuals take the time to do so. Possibly because, were it explained, and therefore comprehended, the average person would have such a grasp of the whole set up that they would protest the current rules of lending and loan repayment procedure and thus by sheer demand in numbers cause a change in these affairs, or, worse yet, understand the rules well enough to actually get ahead and succeed on the subject of home ownership. At the very least, one can agree, that for some reason, those in the know generally do not take the time to promote the system as the truly simple thing it is, and thus put you, the home buyer, at ease, in control and at the advantage regarding your home buying situation.

This book is set up with lots of examples, so that the information given is not just a lot of meaningless words that are difficult to relate to anything real. The figures given in these examples are very real, and are designed to give a visual and graphic reality on the theory and facts behind the workings of a loan. In reading this book, should you find that you "know it all already," then I can assume that your own loan or loans are being paid down at rates with which you are pleased and you are more than likely satisfied with their progress and your personal achievements for your loans. In that case, I urge you to give this book to someone you know who could profit from the information in the book, and themselves get as causative over their loan as you undoubtedly already are over yours. It may seem like a small thing to do for someone, but, I assure you, for those who haven't the vaguest idea of how to be in control of their mortgage loan so that they can achieve greater equity, increase their net worth, and achieve home ownership faster and much less expensively, it will be a gift they can use.

Although this book was originally written when interest rates were quite a bit higher than they are now, the principles of how loans work, how to pay them off faster and less expensively and how to control the payoff of your own loan are the same. Once you get the theory and see examples of it in practical application, as I have given you here, that same data can be applied to any loan amount, any interest rate, any term, and any situation.

I have found that the thing folks most want in life is to achieve an understanding of whatever it is they are dealing with because with that understanding they can do so many things, not to mention that it just plain feels good to understand something. Within the pages of this book, it is my hope that you are brought to an understanding of the Truth in Lending, and that with that understanding you can achieve with your loans what you want to achieve, and that you, the individual, are all the wiser for having an understanding of it.

PART 1
THE TRUTH

Chapter 1-1
General Information

You may or may not know this, but on an average, a home buyer will spend approximately three to four times the amount they borrow to repay a home loan under the current system of banking. For example, on a loan of $100,000 at 10% over 30 years, a home buyer will actually repay $315,928.80. On a loan of, say, $300,000 at 10%, a 30 year loan will cost the home buyer very close to $1,000,000 for that home.

This is an expensive way to buy a home, and, in fact, this amount of expense in home buying is a relatively new idea. "New and improved" loan ideas which actually put the reality of HOME OWNERSHIP into a far away category are unnecessary, and, in fact, oppressive to the home buyer. That is my opinion, and a banker may have a very different opinion of it, but I, for one, am more in the 'home buyer' category than the lender category.

This book, therefore, is not so much about HOME BUYING as it is about HOME OWNERSHIP, a thing of which I am a great proponent. But, in this day and age, and under the present popular forms of mortgage loans, one has to know something about home buying in order to achieve home ownership.

Although millions of people buy homes every year in this country, few know enough about the subject to make the necessary financial judgments that will make that home purchase a viable activity for themselves and their children. In actual fact, the basics of this subject are very simple to learn and understand, and some of those basic facts are what this book is all about. I am personally an advocate of people being able to own their own homes, lock, stock and barrel, and not having to stretch that home buying procedure over 20, 30 or 40 years. And I know that the easiest and best way to do that is to educate people on some of the various, simple ways they can bring this about. I don't believe that people should be left in the dark, but that they should be brought to a new awareness and understanding, so that they can determine their own future. That is the goal of this book, and if it brings you closer to it, then I will have achieved my purpose.

Chapter 1-2
30 Year Fixed Rate Loan

The most common, and one of the most expensive types of loans in this country, is the thirty year fixed rate loan. Under this type of loan, one gets a certain loan amount (the principal), and to that amount is added a certain amount of interest. Let's say that the loan amount is $100,000, and the fixed interest rate is 10%, using these figures for ease in demonstration. Calculating the total amount you would pay for that loan, and your monthly or yearly decreasing principal, is an arduous process when doing it by hand but we'll go through it here briefly so you understand how it is that your loan payments and decreasing principal balance are figured at the lender's end. Those of you to whom this basic data is already well understood, bear with me here. You may yet find some items of information that are of interest to you and can be of assistance in becoming more 'savvy' in terms of just what the best way to pay off your own loan is.

To calculate the first month's information, take $100,000 and multiply it by .10.

$$\$100,000 \times .10 = \$10,000$$

This gives you the amount of interest you'd pay on that loan in one year IF your principal balance remained at $100,000 for the entire year, which of course, it doesn't. This calculation will, however, give you the amount of your first month's interest. Take that $10,000 and divide it by 12 months. That is:

$$\$10,000 \div 12 = \$833.33$$

The answer is the amount in interest you will pay on your $100,000 loan in the first month of your payments. Payments on a $100,000 loan over 30 years at 10% are $877.57 per month (excluding any additional payments you send your lender for tax and insurance escrows), so, of the $877.57 monthly payment on your loan, for the first month, $833.33 of this goes to the lender towards your interest on the loan, and the remaining $44.24 goes towards principal. So, after one month of payments, your principal loan balance is now $99,955.76.

Let's take the second month. Your loan balance is now $99,955.76. Again, multiply this figure by 10%, which will give you the total interest remaining to be paid for the year with this new loan balance, and then, again, divide that number by 12 months:

$$\$99,955.76 \times .10 = \$9,995.57$$

$$\$9,995.57 \div 12 = \$832.96$$

This is the amount of your second month's payment that will go towards owed interest on your loan. The balance of your payment will reduce your principal. Let's calculate it out.

$$\$877.57 - \$832.96 = \$44.61$$

In the second month of payments, your principal loan amount has been reduced by $44.61, so your loan balance now would be $99,911.15.

Here is a table to give you an overview of the first two years of payments on this loan:

Pmt	Payment	Interest	Principal	Balance
1	$877.57	$833.33	$44.24	$99,955.76
2	$877.57	$832.96	$44.61	$99,911.15
3	$877.57	$832.59	$44.98	$99,866.17
4	$877.57	$832.32	$45.35	$99,820.82
5	$877.57	$831.84	$45.73	$99,775.09
6	$877.57	$831.46	$46.11	$99,728.98
7	$877.57	$831.07	$46.50	$99,682.48
8	$877.57	$830.69	$46.88	$99,635.60
9	$877.57	$830.30	$47.27	$99,588.33
10	$877.57	$829.90	$47.67	$99,540.66

Pmt	Payment	Interest	Principal	Balance
11	$877.57	$829.51	$48.06	$99,492.14
12	$877.57	$829.11	$48.46	$99,444.14
Totals	$10,530.84	$9,974.97	$555.87	$99,444.14

Pmt	Payment	Interest	Principal	Balance
13	$877.57	$828.70	$48.87	$99,395.27
14	$877.57	$828.29	$49.28	$99,345.99
15	$877.57	$827.88	$49.69	$99,296.30
16	$877.57	$827.47	$50.10	$99,246.20
17	$877.57	$827.05	$50.52	$99,195.68
18	$877.57	$826.63	$50.94	$99,144.74
19	$877.57	$826.21	$51.36	$99,093.38
20	$877.57	$825.78	$51.79	$99,041.59
21	$877.57	$825.35	$52.22	$98,989.37
22	$877.57	$824.91	$52.66	$98,936.71
23	$877.57	$824.47	$53.10	$98,883.61
24	$877.57	$824.03	$53.54	$98,830.07
Totals	$10,530.84	$9,916.77	$614.07	$98,830.07

By this table, you can see that after two years of payments totaling $21,061.68, the equity you have put into your home by way of your payments, (that is, excluding any appreciation value, home improvement value, etc.) is $1,169.94. The balance of those payments, or $19,891.74, went toward interest on your loan.

Now, let's look at the middle of this loan. This is year 15:

Pmt	Payment	Interest	Principal	Balance
169	$877.57	$699.22	$178.35	$83,728.03
170	$877.57	$697.73	$179.84	$83,548.19
171	$877.57	$696.23	$181.34	$83,366.85
172	$877.57	$694.72	$182.85	$83,184.00
173	$877.57	$693.20	$184.37	$82,999.63
174	$877.57	$691.66	$185.91	$82,813.72
175	$877.57	$690.11	$187.46	$82,626.26
176	$877.57	$688.55	$189.02	$82,437.24
177	$877.57	$686.98	$190.59	$82,246.65
178	$877.57	$685.39	$192.18	$82,054.47
179	$877.57	$683.79	$193.78	$81,860.69
180	$877.57	$682.17	$195.40	$81,665.29
Totals	$10,530.84	$8,289.75	$2,241.09	$81,665.29

Totals to Date:

Payments	Interest Paid	Principal Paid	Balance
$157,962.60	$139,627.74	$18,334.86	$81,665.29

The 'paid in' equity in your home is now $18,334.86. You have

paid $157,962.60 so far on your loan and of that, $139,627.74 has

been paid towards interest. As you can see from the charts, as time

goes on and the principal decreases even slightly, the amount of your payment that is put towards interest decreases slightly, and the amount going to pay off your principal increases slightly, so that by year 15, about $185 each month is going towards your principal loan payment, as compared with about $46 in your first year of payments. There is an end to this, but, as you can see, by and large, the interest is paid first.

Look at year 30, the last year of your loan:

Pmt	Payment	Interest	Principal	Balance
349	$877.57	$83.21	$794.36	$9,191.16
350	$877.57	$76.59	$800.98	$8,390.18
351	$877.57	$69.92	$807.65	$7,582.53
352	$877.57	$63.19	$814.38	$6,768.15
353	$877.57	$56.40	$821.17	$5,946.98
354	$877.57	$49.56	$828.01	$5,118.97
355	$877.57	$42.66	$834.91	$4,284.06
356	$877.57	$35.70	$841.87	$3,442.19
357	$877.57	$28.68	$848.89	$2,593.30
358	$877.57	$21.61	$855.96	$1,737.34
359	$877.57	$14.48	$863.09	$874.25
360	$877.57	3.32	$874.25	$0.00
Totals	$10,530.84	$545.32	$9.985.22	$0.00

30 Year Totals:			
Payments	Interest Paid	Principal Paid	Balance
$315,925.20	$215,925.20	$100,000	$0.00

When I've first shown people how this actually works, they find their hair standing on end. It's not that the information is hidden. When one goes to settlement on a loan, it is required by law that the lender disclose to the purchaser or borrower exactly how much they will be paying on their loan in total payments and in total interest payments. So the information is made known to the home buyer, whether he or she cares to digest the information at that point or not. What often is not made clear is exactly how the loan amortization works. And it is for that reason that people often don't know exactly what, if anything, they can do about the situation. However, it is my experience that with understanding comes the knowledge necessary to get one out of a situation they find unfavorable and the ability to change what they want changed about a situation. It is for this reason that I have spent time on this basic demonstration of how a normal loan is amortized. I will show you some ways to save tens, even hundreds of thousands of dollars, on your total interest payments in succeeding chapters of this book which you can use and implement yourself. But the best guarantee of actually saving those tens or hundreds of thousands of dollars is by increasing your own understanding of loans, loan payments, interest, and principal reductions, and how these work.

Chapter 1-3
Interest Rates

Many people don't realize just how much difference a few percentage points in the interest rate can mean to both their monthly payment and the overall amount they will be paying for their loan. The best way for this information to become clear is by graphic example, so I'll give you some simple comparisons here.

Let's say that you have a 30 year fixed rate loan of $275,000 at 6%. Your monthly payment on this loan would be $2,012.71 and your total payments would be $593,557. Of that, $318,557 would be interest payments on your loan. What are the differences in, say, a point lower or a point or two higher? Let's look at it. We'll compare the monthly payment, the monthly interest and the total payments (principal and interest combined) over the life of the loan on a $275,000 loan at 5%, 6%, 7% and 8% in the chart which follows.

Loan Amount	Interest Rate	Monthly Payment	Total Interest	Total Payments
$275,000	5%	$1476.26	$256,453	$531,453
$275,000	6%	2012.71	$318,557	$593,557
$275,000	7%	$1829.58	$383,651	$658,651
$275,000	8%	$2017.85	$451,430	$726,430

As you can see, both the monthly payments and the overall payments are quite different with these percentage point changes. That is to be expected. But look at this: Loan Amount: $275,000

Pmt #	Interest Rate	Monthly Payment	Amount of Payment Put Towards Principal
1	5%	$1476.26	$330.43
1	6%	$1,648.76	$273.76
1	7%	$1,829.58	$225.41
1	8%	$2,017.85	$184.52
12	5%	$1,476.26	$345.89
12	6%	$1,648.76	$289.20
12	7%	$1,829.58	$240.31
12	8%	$2,017.85	$198.51
24	5%	$1,476.26	$363.59
24	6%	$1,648.76	$307.04
24	7%	$1,829.58	$257.68
24	8%	$2,017.85	$214.98

As you can see, the higher your interest rate, and thus the higher your monthly payment as above, the less of that payment is actually going towards reducing your principal balance for the first many years of your loan. Comparing a 5% interest rate with a 6% interest rate as above, even though your monthly payment is higher with a 6% loan, the amount going towards actually reducing your principal loan balance is lower. It isn't until the 20th year of payments at 6% that the amount of your payment that is applied towards your loan balance becomes higher than the amount taken from a 5% monthly payment amount. That extra amount you have been paying is interest. Here's another example using a higher loan amount of $525,000.

Pmt #	Interest Rate	Monthly Payment	Amount of Payment Put Towards Principal
1	5%	$2,818.31	$630.81
1	6%	$3,147.64	$522.64
1	7%	$3,492.84	$430.34
1	8%	$3,852.26	$352.26
12	5%	$2,818.31	$660.33
12	6%	$3147.64	$552.11
12	7%	$3,492.84	$458.77
12	8%	$3,852.26	$378.97

Pmt #	Interest Rate	Monthly Payment	Amount of Payment Put Towards Principal
24	5%	$2,818.31	$694.12
24	6%	$3,147.64	$586.17
24	7%	$3,492.84	$491.94
24	8%	$3,852.26	$410.43

Comparing payments on this loan amount at 5% versus payments at 6%, again, although the monthly payment is higher at 6% than it is at 5%, the amount of that payment going towards reducing the principal loan amount is less in the 6% payment than it is in the 5% payment. This holds true until the last month of the 14th year of payments. Let's look at total payments on this loan:

Interest Rate	Monthly Payment	Total Interest	Total Payments
5%	$2,818.31	$489,594	$1,014,594
6%	$3,147.64	$608,150	$1,133,150
7%	$3,492.84	$732,422	$1,257,422
8%	$3,852.26	$861,819	$1,386,819

As you can see, for a $525,000 loan, the total payments are almost $300,000 higher on a 7% loan than they are on a 4.5% loan. The payments are more than $90,000 more on a 6% loan than they are with a 5% loan. However, the difference in the amount of the monthly payments can often make a difference in whether a person can even qualify for a loan at a given rate and comfortably make the payments for that rate. We'll go further into the subject of interest rates in subsequent sections of the book.

Chapter 1-4
Adjustable Rate Loans
Flexible Payments and Option ARMs
and Negative Amortization

An Adjustable Rate Loan is just that. The interest rate on the loan adjusts periodically. This adjustment can occur daily, monthly, yearly, or in just about any interval one can imagine. The adjustment can be based on an agreed upon rate of adjustment at the time the loan is made, it can be based on the changing market, it can be based on a certain fixed percentage above prime rate. In short, it can mean many things, but the most important thing about an adjustable rate loan is that you understand how and when it adjusts so you can track your current interest rate, your current payment, and your declining loan balance yourself, because, while this type of loan has its merits, it also has its pitfalls. They are simple to understand, but you must watch for them.

Let's take a simple 30 year loan that is adjusting yearly. Let's say the initial interest rate is 4.5%, to adjust up one interest point yearly to a maximum of 8.5%. The loan amount is $350,000. This will give you low monthly payments in the early years of the loan, but as time goes on, your payments should be increasing along with your interest rate increases. Let's take a look at how this loan would look.

Your monthly payments on this loan would look like this:

Year	Monthly Payments
1 (4.5%)	$1,773.40
2 (5.5%)	$1,981.90
3 (6.5%)	$2,195.88
4 (7.5%)	$2,414.21
5 (8.5%)	$2,635.88

The $2,635.88 monthly payment would then continue for the remainder of the loan.

Your yearly totals would look like this during the adjustable period:

Year	Int. Rate	Yearly Payments	Yearly Interest	Yearly Principal
1	4.5%	$21,280.80	$15,634.49	$5,646.31
2	5.5%	$23,782.80	$18,805.48	$4,967.32
3	6.5%	$26,350.56	$21,929.94	$4,420.62
4	7.5%	$28,970.52	$24,987.37	$3,983.15
5	8.5%	$31,630.56	$27,994.02	$3,636.54

In the case of this particular loan the rate has adjusted such that your total yearly principal payments are decreasing over the first 5 years of the loan. Out of a total of $112,915.24 paid during the first five years of this loan, the amount of principal paid down of the initial $350,000 borrowed is only $22,653.94. In the ensuing years, of course, equity will start increasing with each passing year by a little at first, and eventually by quite a lot, until the term of your loan is up and your loan is paid in full. But, for now, the amount you are spending yearly on your mortgage payments increases as the interest rate increases, while the amount of your payment going towards decreasing your loan balance is less with each passing year. This can be rather depressing as you work harder and harder each year to keep up with your increasing monthly payment amount.

Let's look at another possible pitfall on an adjustable rate mortgage. Let's say our loan is for $455,000 at an initial interest rate of 4%, the rate to adjust annually at 1% above prime, with a maximum monthly payment of $2,512.53. Your monthly payments in the beginning would be $2,172.24, which is the standard payment on a $455,000 loan over 30 years at 4%, and your payments adjust upwards as your interest rate increases to the maximum of $2,512.53. Your payments can never go higher than this amount, and this monthly payment fits into your budget, so everything is fine, right? Well, not necessarily. That $2,512.53 per month is the usual payment for a $455,000 loan over 30 years at 5.25%. What happens if your interest rate hits 7%? You get off easy, right? Wrong. Let's look at one way this loan could go.

Let's say that the loan started out at 4%. After one year the rate increased to 5% for 12 months, and then to 6% for one year, at which point it hit 7%. At a monthly maximum payment of $2,512.53, your payment each month will not even cover the interest on your remaining balance at 7% What happens then? Simple. Whatever is not paid to cover interest each month is simply added to your outstanding principal balance. In this case, then, we have what is called a NEGATIVE AMORTIZATION. This is where, due to the above situation, your principal balance is not decreasing with each monthly payment you make, it is increasing.

Remember, at the end of the 3rd year, your interest rate was 6%, which put your balance at that point at $433,703.46. Then the 7%

rate kicked in. Payments at 7% on a remaining balance of $433,703.46 should be $2,983.08 to pay both the interest and give some over to the principal. But you're paying only $2,512.53. Look at what happens in the first year of payments on this schedule.

Pmt #	Payment	Interest	Principal	Balance
37	$2,512.53	$2,529.94	- $17.41	$433,720.87
38	$2,512.53	$2,583.09	- $34.92	$433,738.38
39	$2,512.53	$2,583.15	- $52.53	$433,755.99
40	$2,512.53	$2,583.22	- $70.24	$433,773.70
41	$2,512.53	$2,583.29	-$88.06	$433,791.52
42	$2,512.53	$2,583.37	-$105.98	$433,809.44
43	$2,512.53	$2,583.44	-$124.01	$433,827.47
44	$2,512.53	$2,583.51	-$142.14	$433,845.60
45	$2,512.53	$2,583.58	-$160.38	$433,863.84
46	$2,512.53	$2,583.66	-$178.72	$433,882.18
47	$2,512.53	$2,583.74	-$197.17	$433,900.63
48	$2,512.53	$2,583.81	-$215.73	$433,919.19

As you can see, your principal balance has increased by $215.17 in this year. What happens then by the end of the term?

Pmt #	Payment	Interest	Principal	Balance
349	$2,512.53	$2,619.39	-$15,442.53	$449,145.99
350	$2,512.53	$2,620.02	-$15,550.02	$449,253.48
351	$2,512.53	$2,620.65	-$15,658.14	$449,361.60

Pmt #	Payment	Interest	Principal	Balance
352	$2,512.53	$2,621.28	-$15,766.89	$449,470.35
353	$2,512.53	$2,621.91	-$15,876.27	$449,579.73
354	$2,512.53	$2,622.55	-$15,986.29	$449,689.75
355	$2,512.53	$2,623.19	-$16,096.95	$449,800.41
356	$2,512.53	$2,623.84	-$16,208.26	$449,911.72
357	$2,512.53	$2,624.49	-$16,320.22	$450,023.68
358	$2,512.53	$2,625.14	-$16,432.83	$450,136.29
359	$2,512.53	$2,625.80	-$16,546.10	$450,249.56
360	$452,872.20	$2,626.46	-$450,249.56	$452,872.20

Because your term is 360 months, anything still due at the end of that term would come due and payable at that time, in this case, $452,876.20, a balance very close to that of your original loan amount, despite that you just spent the last 30 years paying very nearly one million dollars in loan (mostly interest) payments. The one million dollars paid does not count the balloon payment of $452,876.20 due at the end of the term.

Now, it is unlikely that an adjustable interest rate would climb to 7% and stay there for the duration of the loan. I used this example to show you the basics of how a negative amortization works and how it can come about. If you have an adjustable rate mortgage, be sure you understand the terms and what interest rate you're paying so you don't get into this situation. And, please don't think it doesn't or hasn't happened. It does, and, unfortunately, has. In fact, with home prices increasing as they have been, creative financing options such as the ones mentioned here have become more and more popular. One can now get a loan known as an Option ARM, or a Flexible Payment ARM. This type of loan states that a homebuyer can decide on a monthly basis how much they want to pay on their loan. It is important that anyone opting for such a loan fully understands the potential ramifications of the various scenarios and be prepared to deal with the ones which do arise. If you have this type of loan, make sure that you understand the examples of negative amortization given above so you don't find yourself in a similar situation.

On some adjustable rate mortgages, you will have a fixed monthly payment, and the thing that changes each month or year along with the interest rate, is the amount of that payment that will go towards interest vs. the amount that will be applied to your principal. For instance, if an adjustable rate loan of $200,000 starts at 5%, adjusts monthly, and has a fixed monthly payment of $1342.05, watch what would happen with your monthly principal payments as this fixed payment loan adjusted:

Pmt #	Monthly Payment	Interest Rate	Interest	Principal
1	$1342.05	5%	$1041.67	$300.38
2	$1342.05	5.125	$1066.43	$275.62
3	$1342.05	5.25%	$1091.23	$250.82
4	$1342.05	5.5%	$1142.04	$200.01
5	$1342.05	5.75%	$1193.00	$149.05
6	$1342.05	6%	$1244.12	$97.93
7	$1342.05	6%	$1243.63	$98.42
8	$1342.05	6.25%	$1294.94	$47.11
9	$1342.05	6.25%	$1294.69	$47.36
10	$1342.05	6.5%	$1346.22	-$4.17
11	$1342.05	6.25%	$1294.47	$47.58
12	$1342.05	6.5%	$1345.99	-$3.94
13	$1342.05	6.5%	$1346.01	-$3.96
14	$1342.05	6.75%	$1397.80	-$55.75
15	$1342.05	6.5%	$1346.33	-$4.28

This example covers the first 15 months on a loan adjusting monthly with a fixed monthly payment. As you can see, the amounts being applied towards your interest, and therefore your principal is what adjusts along with your interest rate, as opposed to your monthly payment adjusting. As $1,342.05 is the monthly payment for a $250,000, 30-year loan at 5%, then, here again, if your interest rate rises above about 6.5% with this monthly payment, you would again be in a negative amortization mode. Option ARM's fall into this category where the home buyer is the one who actually decides how much he wants to pay each month. Where the payment amount falls short of owned interest for the month, that home buyer is increasing, not decreasing, the amount he will ultimately owe on his loan.

This type of loan can have advantages, as you can see, but the advantages definitely depend upon the fluctuating market. Once again, you can see that a difference of a few interest points makes a lot of difference on how quickly your loan is being paid down.

There are as many things to say about adjustable rate mortgages as there are different types of these loans. It would be impossible to detail every type of adjustable rate mortgage available and just as needless. If you know what the terms of your loan are, and have a pretty good idea of the estimated or projected rate of change of the interest rate, the details of your loan can be figured out for you using any amortization calculators. These exist on-line and in small hand-held calculator form and can be invaluable in tracking the progress of your loan and in making decisions relating to paying it down, refinancing, etc. You can also buy software that will allow you to track your progress completely. And, after a short time of applying some of the solutions contained in Part 2 of this book, you will be able to track your progress on your own, with or without calculators. So, for now, just read and digest the general information on loan workings.

Chapter 1-5
Interest Only Loans

With the rapid rise in home prices, new and first time home buyers are increasingly in the market to find financing they can afford. This has sometimes been called "creative financing." Creative financing now comes in many more forms than ever before. In this chapter, we are going to look at two of those forms.

A popular form of financing is Interest Only Financing. With this form of loan, a mortgage is structured such that the home buyer pays only interest on his loan each month for a certain, specified period of time. After this specified period of time, he either begins making standard payments on the loan or pays the entire balance of interest plus principal in one lump sum. This lump payment is called a balloon payment. As an example, the home buyer may pay interest only on his loan for the first 5 years of the loan. During this time the interest rate may be fixed or may vary, depending on the terms of his agreement. After five years, the loan usually either converts to a standard loan now amortizing over 25 years with a variable rate or one is required to pay off the loan in one large payment. Another option at this point would be to obtain new financing.

The interest only loan has been around for years and was a popular loan in the 20's until the Great Depression hit, at which time many could no longer pay their loans and bank foreclosures forced people to lose their homes entirely. Over the last several decades interest only loans have been used largely by a person getting a temporary loan for construction purposes or for the financing of investment properties. Now, however, these loans have made a comeback because they enable folks to purchase a home they otherwise would not be able to afford. These loans are designed to reduce the monthly outlay in the early years of the loan and they do, in fact, save the homebuyer a degree of financial outlay as he is paying only interest in the first months or years of his loan and is not paying down the principal at all. The following chart will show you three different loan amounts, each at 6% interest. You can see what the interest only monthly payment of each would be and the amount one would not be paying in principal each month to try and keep the monthly payment in an affordable range.

Loan Amount	Initial Interest Rate	Monthly Payment (Interest Only)	Principal Payment Not Made (Deferred)	Equity Accumulated During Interest Only Payments
$250,000	6%	$1250.00	$248.88	$0
$375,000	6%	$1875.00	$373.31	$0
$500,000	6%	$2500.00	$497.75	$0

In each case above, the Principal Payment Not Made column shows the amount of owed principal being deferred under the Interest Only loan obligation expires. The loss of accumulated equity, or ownership, in the home shows up in the consistently $0 total in the last column until such point as the loan structure reverts to a standard interest plus principal payment or until the balloon payment is made at the end of the interest only period. Some new home buyers find that by paying Interest Only for the first months or years of their loan, they can more easily afford the payments on their home loan. In the $250,000 example above, the home buyer is paying $248.88 less each month by deferring the amount which would ordinarily be his principal payment for the month. In the $375,000 example, the amount being deferred is $373.31, so his payment is $1,875.00 rather than $2,248.31.

Although the loans are advertised as enabling the home buyer to save the difference in payments, this is actually a misnomer, as he is only deferring payment to a later date, not actually saving this money.

Despite the fact that there is no equity buildup being accumulated with this loan structure, there are instances where this loan makes sense and which distinguishes it from continuing to simply pay rent to someone else. During periods of rapidly rising home prices, one's equity in their home is increasing without ever making a principal reducing payment. If, during the initial 5 year interest only payment period, one's home value increases, let us say, from a purchase price of $350,000 to a market value of $500,000, the home purchaser has achieved a $150,000 increase in equity value while making interest only payments. If the home buyer could only qualify for the $350,000 loan based on monthly payments of interest only, this would not be a bad investment and would place the homebuyer in a position of being able to buy a home in a rapidly rising market before housing prices got so out of hand he or she never would be able to catch up to the accelerating cost of a mortgage. In other words, if the home buyer, knowing he couldn't really afford the payments on a standard $350,000 mortgage, were to decide to wait a few years while working to increase his income, in a few years that same home may well be selling for $500,000 and he would still be trying to get in a position to buy a home. By opting for the interest only loan in the first place, he has gotten into a position of being able to buy a home he could not otherwise afford, while working to increase his ability to pay for it, all the while gaining market driven equity in the home.

This is a bit speculative and somewhat risky but there is and always has been money to be made in speculation by those willing to take a chance on real estate. What is new about this is not the fact of real estate speculation, but the fact that Harry Home Buyer is taking part in speculation for a chance to become Harry Home Owner, whereas this degree of risk has traditionally been undertaken in the main by investors. Housing prices can suddenly fall and income expectations can fall short making an investment via an Interest Only Loan somewhat risky when you're talking about one's primary residence. On the other hand, no one gets anywhere without taking at least some risk and, let's face it, any mortgage has built into it some degree of risk, as no one knows for certain how their lives or the markets will unfold over the length of any loan.

Avoiding all risk is not possible in life or home ownership. Life has risks, that is a fact that is not going to go away. Understanding the risks of an undertaking and having a plan in any eventuality is more the object here and that is why it is important when obtaining a mortgage to completely understand that mortgage inside and out. And don't forget that even during the interest only payment years of the loan one can make a principal payment. Every dollar you pay in principal is a dollar you won't be paying interest on for the remainder of the loan's term. And once the interest only loan option expires and you are making regularly amortized loan payments, all of the information in the second part of this book applies. So, the message soon to come is that even with an Interest Only loan, there is still a way you can own your home sooner and for less money. Read on.

Chapter 1-6
Points

Just what are "points," and how did they come into being? It is important to spend a little time covering this subject, as you will be charged points of some kind on almost any mortgage you get whether they are advertised as "points" or whether they are hidden in amongst the closing costs you pay when you go to settle on your loan.

Points are simply this: a point is an amount of money equal to 1% of the amount of your loan. Points are additional fees you pay the lender. There are two primary types of fees charged in terms of points. One is the 'Loan Origination Fee,' and the other is called a 'Loan Discount Fee.'

The loan origination fee, usually one or two points, or 1% or 2% of your loan amount, is a fee charged by the bank for giving you the loan. It is an administrative charge. This is one way the bank makes money on your loan. Sometimes you can find a loan with no points, or fees, charged, and these loans generally carry a higher interest rate than loans with fees.

Loan discount fees vary depending on the market and the type of loan obtained, but are fees charged by the lender when he is giving you a particularly low interest rate, or a "discounted" interest rate. It is how the lender makes money on your loan up-front. It's a trade-off - you pay a higher interest rate and no discount points, or you get a lower rate but you pay "points" or a lump sum of money to the lender instead, quite in addition to the principal loan amount you are borrowing from him. So, again, points are simply added fees of one type or another charged by the lender in giving you your loan.

What, you might ask, about all the money being made in interest on my loan? Look here, I'm borrowing $100,000 and this lender is making $215,000 profit in interest payments. What about that? Why am I being charged other fees in lending me this money?

Well, you're right, in a sense. Someone is making $215,000 on your loan, but it isn't the bank. It used to be that that was the business the bank was in. You'd go to a bank and borrow some money and they'd charge you X percent interest and you'd pay it and you'd get your house and they'd make their money and as long as you paid it through to the end, that was the end of it.

Well, that was the old days. That's not how loans typically unfold in this day and age. What happens today is that you apply for a loan, the bank charges you a loan origination fee and, sometimes, loan discount points for this loan. They give you the money, and then the bank sells your loan on the secondary market. Loans are usually sold to one of two corporations, Fannie Mae or Freddie Mac, which, in their turn, sell the loan to investors.

The bank you borrowed from no longer holds the note but, nonetheless, continues to collect your payments from you and keeps track of your loan for you. The bank you originally borrowed the money from, having resold it on the secondary market, now has that money back right away. They've made some profit on it as they've collected your loan origination fee from you. They may also have collected from you a loan discount fee.

If you were charged loan discount fees, then it can be assumed you obtained a relatively low interest rate. As you were given a discounted rate, and your lender now has to re-sell this loan on the secondary market, he will get less for your loan when he resells it than he would get for a higher interest rate loan. As your lender wants to resell the loan so as to recapture cold cash for it right away rather than having to wait 20, 30 or 40 years for the money at $877.57 per month, he is willing to sell it at such a discount. The money he has recouped can now be lent to other borrowers.

So, the loan discount points are designed to offset the difference in the interest rate charged on your loan vs. the amount your lender will be able to get for the loan when he resells it. With a low interest rate, he has lost much of the profit he will make on the sale of your loan and so makes up for this by charging you fees in exchange for the lower interest rate.

The number of points varies with the lending institution and the particular loan you get. They can be as high as 3 or 4 points for a loan origination fee, and as high as 14 points for loan discount fees, which, in the case of $100,000 loan would be $3,000-$4,000 up front from you at the time of settlement in loan origination fees, and more for loan discount fees. On a $300,000 loan, 3 or 4 points would be $9,000-$12,000.

Generally, the lower your interest rate, the higher your loan discount points. Sometimes a bank offers no points and a higher interest rate or a longer term. Which loan would be best at any given time depends on the purchaser's current financial picture, his plans for the loan, how far into this loan payments he is, his intentions to resell or not resell the property after a certain amount of time, his knowledge of how to take that loan and pay it down faster (this topic will be covered later in the book), and various other factors. The thing to do would be to look at your financial picture and plans, and, if desired, get a comparative analysis done on the types of loans offered to help clarify these various options for you.

Chapter 1-7
The 40 Year Mortgage

During the 1990's, some banks came out with the 40-year mortgage. This was designed, presumably, to make it easier for the home buyer to qualify for a loan, reducing their monthly payments by increasing their term. Of course, if you borrow a sum of money with a term of 30 years, your monthly payments would be lower than if you had borrowed that same sum of money for 10 years because the loan amount would be stretched out over a longer period of time. But, just what real advantage this 40-year mortgage is to the home buyer who wants to own his home needs a close inspection.

Let's look at the differences between a 30-year $100,000 loan at 10% vs. the same loan over 40 years.

Loan Amount: $100,000

Interest Rate: 10%

Terms: 30 years and 40 years

Term	Monthly Payment	Total Interest	Total Payments
30 years	$877. 57	$215,925.20	$315,925.20
40 years	$848.15	$307,592.00	$407,592.00

The 40-year mortgage was promoted as a new solution to the expense of a 30-year loan by extending the term of the loan and thus lowering its monthly payment. But, as you can see in the above example, the monthly payment on a 40-year loan is only $28.42 less than on a 30 year loan. By and large, the rest of the money one is paying is interest, for 10 additional years.

There can be some advantages on the loan origination fee side of the loan, as some 40-year loans offer no points. This can save a homeowner a good deal of money up front, especially if his loan is a rather large one. Points of 1% of the loan amount on a $400,000 loan, with the bank charging 3 or 4 points, is $12,000-$16,000 down, quite in addition to the down payment for the property. So that could be an advantage. In that instance, let's look at the borrower's overall payments both ways.

Loan Amount: $400,000 (0 Points)

Interest Rate: 10%

Term: 40 years

Monthly Payment	Total Paid	Total Interest Paid
$3,396.58	$1,630,358.40	$1,230,358.40

Let's compare that with a 30-year loan with points.

Loan Amount: $400,000 (3 Points)

Interest Rate: 10%

Term: 30 years

Monthly Payment	Total Paid	Total Interest Paid
$3,510.29	$1,263,704.40	$863,704.40

In this example, if you look at the difference in the monthly payments between a 30-year loan and a 40-year loan, you will see that the difference is only $113.71 a month. Yet, because payments of $3,396.58 are being made for ten additional years, the payments made total $366,654 more on a 40-year loan than on a 30-year loan. That's $366,654 more in interest payments to save $113.71 a month in one's monthly payment, or to save $12,000 in points. Well, the truth is that in some situations, all one can do is go with the longer term and 0 points.

Fortunately, there is something that can be done even about this. One alternative, of course, is to finance the points in with the loan, which can often be done in a refinancing situation. A $12,000 loan over 30 years would be a total loan repayment of around $37,000. That's a lot less than the $366,654 put out in 10 additional years of interest. Most people could find something to do with that $329,654 they saved in interest payments.

These are just a few examples and possible alternatives. There are actually many alternatives, and that's what we're just about to get to here.

PART II
SOME SOLUTIONS

Chapter 2-1
General Information

If the information contained in the first section of this book was new to you and hasn't knocked you over yet, then you will find the information in the second section of this book greatly relieving. This section of the book covers some solutions to the way most loans are structured in this country and should help to put you at cause over your own loan payments and give you a feeling of accomplishment every time you pay down a part of your loan faster.

Paying down a loan faster than the way it was set up to be paid is not a difficult thing to do, and it can be done in such a way that you know what you are doing with your loan and have prediction on how much progress you are making in doing so.

Paying off your loan faster and less expensively can be done even if you don't generally have a lot of money left at the end of your month, and, if you want to badly enough, even if you usually have more month left at the end of your money.

In this section of the book, I will give you some ways in which this can be done without a lot of sophisticated computers or software, but with just what information you have so far discovered for yourself by gaining an understanding of the way most loans are structured. Or, you can figure the best way to pay off your loan within your own budget or financial means with the assistance of computer analysis supplied to you for a small fee by companies that specialize in this line of work.

Either way, we are over the hurdle of astonishment at how loans work, and are about to enter the body of knowledge which will get you in complete control of your own home mortgage.

This is the fun part of the book.

Chapter 2-2
Bi-Weekly Mortgage Savings

There is a concept which has been out in paying mortgages down, growing in popularity since the late 80's which is very simple to do and quite affordable for the average home buyer. This method of paying one's mortgage can actually save the home buyer tens, and even hundreds of thousands of dollars on his home mortgage. It is commonly referred to as a system of Bi-Weekly Mortgage Payments. The term bi-weekly refers to making one-half your monthly payment every two weeks, rather than a full payment once a month. It works well in this country where 30-year fixed and adjustable rate loans compounded monthly are the norm. It is a workable system and can be done on one's own, or for a fee with the help of companies who offer this sort of service.

Generally, when one mentions a bi-weekly program, he is not referring to mailing in payments bi-weekly, or once every two weeks, to one's lender. Most lenders, in fact, will not arrange one's payments to be due every two weeks because they are not, in the main, set up to do so. Re-systemizing thousands of mortgages just to be able to accept a few bi-weekly payments would be a very expensive undertaking and would not be very cost efficient for the lender, although you can find a few who will accept them. However, unless your loan was set up that way from the start, you would probably find yourself needing to refinance your loan to get onto that system with a lender who offered that type of program. That, then, gets into refinancing costs, more points, etc. and most probably would not be cost efficient for you either.

Most Bi-Weekly Payment Programs currently being offered in this country are based on the simple fact that as little as one extra payment per year on your mortgage will dramatically reduce both the term of your loan as well as the overall amount you will pay for that loan.

When you make one-half a payment every two weeks, rather than one full payment once a month, you are making 26 bi-weekly payments a year. If there were just four weeks in every month then this would not be so. There would be 48 weeks in a year and therefore 24 bi-weekly periods in a year. But, in reality, there are 52 weeks in a year and therefore 26 bi-weekly periods in a year. By either paying or setting aside one-half of your mortgage payment once every two weeks, as opposed to a full payment once a month, you are essentially accumulating one full extra payment a year. Because it is accumulating a little at a time over the full year, it is generally not so painful as trying to come up with a full extra payment all at once at the end of the year when that $1,000 or $2,000 or whatever your mortgage payment amount is would undoubtedly come into good use elsewhere. It is really a simple process, and many people do not realize just what effect one full extra payment per year can have on a home mortgage.

There are several ways one can go about making this one extra payment per year. One way, obviously, is to go ahead and send it in once a year as an extra payment to be applied towards the principal balance.

Another way would be to set aside one-half of your payment every two weeks, make a monthly payment for the usual amount, and take that extra, already-set-aside money which will have accumulated over twelve months, and send it in at the end of the year as a full payment towards principal reduction. As funds set aside in this manner can tend to be used for unexpected expenses or emergencies, a better way might be to calculate out the total amount of 13 payments per year, divide that figure by 12, and make that the amount you send in monthly as your payment, being certain to mark the extra amount 'For Principal Only.'

If you were to make this one extra payment per year from the inception of your loan payments, as a rule of thumb, you would take roughly 9 years off your loan and save a dramatic amount in interest payments. On the $100,000 loan over 30 years, you would save approximately $73,000 in interest payments. Of course, the exact amount of savings would depend not only on the original loan amount, but also on the interest rate you are paying, how far into the loan these extra payments started being made and what the original term of your loan was. To give you some examples, we'll look at some actual facts given to real home buyers on their own home mortgages.

I worked for a time as a mortgage consultant, assisting people with ways to save money on their home loans, and also selling this Bi-Weekly system of mortgage reduction when needed. In the first couple of weeks of this work, I showed area homeowners how to save interest payments totaling over 3.75 million dollars on their existing home loans. Most of the analysis at that time was done comparing their standard payment schedule with that of getting onto a bi-weekly system of payments which would guarantee them an extra payment per year and the savings that went with it.

Some actual savings examples from that time period are listed below to show you how much can be saved using this system. In each of these examples the loan had an term of 30 years.

Original Loan Amount	Interest Rate	No. Yrs into Loan	Total Bi-Weekly Term	Savings
$102,999	11.019%	1.5 yrs	21.21 yrs	$84,170.83
$280,000	9.75%	0.0 yrs	21.11 yrs	$205,596.86
$400,000	9.5%	0.16 yrs	21.79 yrs	$258,196.08
$ 93,000	9.5%	0.0 yrs	21.72 yrs	$60,710.46
$428,000	9.5%	1.67 yrs	22.55 yrs	$246,737.38
$ 45,000	8.5%	2.5 yrs	23.15 yrs	$21,278.04
$187,000	10%	0.0 yrs	21.25 yrs	$137,309.12
$187,350	9.875%	2.75 yrs	22.99 yrs	$104,970.81

As you can see, the savings depends on how long the original term is, the original loan amount, the interest rate and how far into the loan one already is when they start this process of additional principal payments. Obviously, the sooner into the loan one begins making additional payments, the greater the savings.

There are companies that are set up specifically to handle your mortgage via Bi-Weekly payment schedules. You sign up for a service with these companies and, for a fee, they will deduct one-half your usual loan payment from your account once every two weeks and send your monthly payment on to your lender as you would. But at the end of one year's time, you would have accumulated in their account one extra full payment that they then send on to your lender for you as well, marked 'For Principal Only.' In this way, your one-half payment every two weeks becomes an expenditure that occurs automatically each month once everything is in place for the debits, and you are assured of a shortened term and enormous savings on your loan. If you're the type of person that spends extra money whenever you have it and would probably not actually make those extra principal payments each month or year, then programs like this are a good idea.

For those of you who would rather do it yourself, the basic data is included above and as soon as you understand it, you can do it

yourself and make it work for you.

Chapter 2-3
Do-It-Yourself-As-Best-You-Can

If you were talking about repairing your dishwasher or plastering a hole in your wall, this might not work out as well as you'd hoped or expected. If you dabble at getting your home appliances to work again and end up leaving major pieces of it out on the kitchen floor, or use the wrong kind of plaster in the hole in the wall, the outcome of 'doing it yourself any old way you can' might not have too appealing an effect for those trying to improve their situation. Fortunately, on the subject of paying off your mortgage or loan faster and saving money on it, you only need to know one thing to get that accomplished. That is, WHEN YOU PAY IT OFF FASTER, YOU PAY IT OFF FASTER.

That's not meant as a joke or as an insult to your intelligence. It is the first thing you need to know when paying off your loan faster. That if you pay it off faster, you will pay it off faster.

Most people know this in a general sort of way, but they often do not know it well enough to use it to pay their loans down faster. As few simple examples will save all the words in the world.

If you had a $100,000 loan at 10% over the 30 years, we know that your payments would be $877.57 per month. What would happen if sent your lender an extra, say, $25 a month, to be applied to your principal only? Let's take a look at it.

If you were to put an extra $25/month towards your principal loan payment every month, you would end up taking over 4 years off your loan and paying $36,661.95 less than you ordinarily would pay. This loan would be paid off in 25.7 years at a total cost of $279,661.95. We'll go through a few of the payments here which you can compare with the $100,000 loan tables in Chapter 1-2 of the first section of this book.

Here are years one and two of this loan, adding $25/month to your payment of $877.57.

Pmt #	Payment	Interest	Principal	Balance
1	$902.57	$833.33	$69.74	$99,930.76
2	$902.57	$832.76	$69.81	$99,860.95
3	$902.57	$832.17	$70.40	$99,730.55

Pmt #	Payment	Interest	Principal	Balance
4	$902.57	$831.59	$70.98	$99,719.57
5	$902.57	$831.00	$71.57	$99,648.00
6	$902.57	$830.40	$72.17	$99,575.83
7	$902.57	$829.80	$72.77	$99,503.06
8	$902.57	$829.19	$73.38	$99,429.68
9	$902.57	$828.58	$73.99	$99,355.69
10	$902.57	$827.96	$74.61	$99,281.08
11	$902.57	$827.34	$75.23	$99,205.85
12	$902.57	$826.72	$75.85	$99,130.00

Yearly Totals:

Payments	Interest Paid	Principal Paid
$10,830.84	$9,960.24	$870.00

Pmt #	Payment	Interest	Principal	Balance
13	$902.57	$826.72	$76.49	$99,053.51
14	$902.57	$825.45	$77.12	$98,976.39
15	$902.57	$824.80	$77.77	$98,898.62
16	$902.57	$824.16	$78.41	$98,820.21
17	$902.57	$823.50	$79.07	$98,741.14
18	$902.57	$822.84	$79.73	$98,661.41
19	$902.57	$822.18	$80.39	$98,581.02
20	$902.57	$821.51	$81.06	$98,499.96

Pmt #	Payment	Interest	Principal	Balance
21	$902.57	$820.83	$81.74	$98,418.22
22	$902.57	$820.15	$82.42	$98,335.80
23	$902.57	$819.47	$83.10	$98,252.70
24	$902.57	$818.77	$83.80	$98,168.90

Yearly Totals:

Payments	Interest Paid	Principal Paid
$10,830.84	$9,869.74	$961.10

Once again, let's jump ahead to year 15 and compare it with year 15 of a standard 30-year payment schedule.

Pmt. #	Payment	Interest	Principal	Balance
169	$902.57	$623.43	$279.14	$74,531.90
170	$902.57	$621.10	$281.47	$74,250.43
171	$902.57	$618.75	$283.82	$73,966.61
172	$902.57	$616.39	$286.18	$73,680.43
173	$902.57	$614.00	$288.57	$73,391.86
174	$902.57	$611.60	$290.97	$73,100.89
175	$902.57	$609.17	$293.40	$72,807.49
176	$902.57	$606.73	$295.84	$72,511.65
177	$902.57	$604.26	$298.31	$72,213.34
178	$902.57	$601.78	$300.79	$71,912.55

Pmt. #	Payment	Interest	Principal	Balance
179	$902.57	$599.27	$303.30	$71,609.25
180	$902.57	$596.74	$305.83	$71,303.42

Yearly Totals:

Payments	Interest Paid	Principal Paid
$10,830.84	$7,323.22	$3,507.62

You can see easily by comparing these two charts that your loan balance here would be over $10,000 less by the end of year 15 than it otherwise would be. That's also $10,000 in additional built up equity in your home by this point in time.

Let's look at the end of your new term, 25 years and 10 months into your loan:

Pmt. #	Payment	Interest	Principal	Balance
299	$902.57	$81.53	$821.04	$8,962.25
300	$902.57	$74.69	$827.88	$8,134.37
301	$902.57	$67.79	$834.78	$7,299.59
302	$902.57	$60.83	$841.74	$6,457.85
303	$902.57	$53.82	$848.75	$5,609.10
304	$902.57	$46.74	$855.83	$4,753.27

Pmt #	Payment	Interest	Principal	Balance
305	$902.57	$39.61	$862.96	$3,890.31
306	$902.57	$32.42	$870.15	$3,020.16
307	$902.57	$25.17	$877.40	$2,142.76
308	$902.57	$17.86	$884.71	$1,258.05
309	$902.57	$10.48	$892.09	$365.96
310	$902.57	$3.16	$365.96	$0.00

Yearly Totals:

Payments	Interest Paid	Principal Paid
$10,830.84	$514.10	$9,783.21

Here, you have paid off your loan 51 months early without hardly even trying. The one thing you must be absolutely certain to do when making an extra principal payment, whether it is $25 or $25,000 is to note, clearly and in writing, along with your additional payment, that you want these funds applied to your principal. Mark it, "For Principal Only." Otherwise, your additional amount will be received and applied towards owed interest on your loan rather than towards reducing your principal loan balance. So this is very important. The major reason that few home buyers make extra principal payments as they can is, truthfully, because few realize just how much of a difference it can make.

Understanding that you can be much more in control of paying down your loan in this way can give that needed, added incentive to make extra principal payments work for you.

Just to give you a few more examples, here is the basic savings data on paying an extra $50/month and an extra $100/month.

Monthly Payment	Years to Pay Off Loan	Total Interest	Total Payments
$927.57 ($50/month extra)	23 yrs	$155,595.55	$255,595.55
$927.57 ($100/month extra)	17.5 yrs	$125,682.00	$225,682.00

You can see here that paying an extra $100 per month on this loan will take 12.5 years off that 30 year loan and save the home buyer over $90,000 in overall interest payments. If one is in a position to do this, and does it religiously, the amount of savings is worth the extra effort. And, remember, you don't have to pay exactly $25 extra every month or $100 extra every month to get ahead at the mortgage game. Every little bit you do, when you can, makes a difference.

All home mortgages must now allow early payoff of some sort by federal law. What you need to watch out for is that there are a few loans that include a penalty for early payoff. Avoid this type of loan if you can, but loans with prepayment penalties are fairly rare anyway; most existing loans allow early payoff with no penalty,

Remember: by paying it down faster, you pay it down faster, and this saves you years of interest payments. In the next few chapters we'll go into why that is so.

Chapter 2-4
Doubling Your Principal Payment

There is a way to cut a 30 year mortgage in half which you can do and monitor very easily yourself.

If you get your loan amortization schedule from your lender, or access it on-line, you will see that it has columns on it detailing your monthly payment, how much of that payment is interest, how much of each payment gets applied to your principal loan balance and what your remaining loan balance is, month by month.

If you were to make your monthly loan payment as requested, and then simply double the amount of your principal payment with each payment you made, you would reduce your term to around 15 years and cut your interest payments in half.

Let's take a $100,000 loan at 10% over 30 years. As covered in the second chapter of this book, this loan paid down in the standard fashion would cost the borrower $315,925.20, of which $215,925.20 is payment of interest on the loan. Let's look at why this is so.

When you borrow that $100,000, remember that we arrived at your first month's interest payment by taking the principal ($100,000), multiplied it by the interest rate (10%) and then divided that figure by 12 months. This gave us a figure of $833.33 for the first month's interest on the loan. Well, did you ever wonder how your principal payment for that first month's payment amount was figured out, or your total monthly principal and interest payment? I'll show you.

You're paying 10% interest, right? So, the $44.24 of your first month's P&I (principal and interest) payment of $877.57 is the amount of money you would have to invest at 10% for 30 years to accrue $833.33 in interest, compounded monthly. So when you are paying that $44.24 in that first month, you are also paying to your lender, at the same time, his 30 years of interest for lending you that $44.24.

In the second month (and you can refer to the table in Chapter 1-2 if you need to), you are still making a monthly payment of $877.57, of which $832.96 is interest, and $44.61 goes towards reducing your principal.

Again, $44.61 is the amount you would need to invest at 10% over 29 years and 11 months to gain $832.96 in interest.

Based on the theory of compounded interest and mortgage loan repayments as discussed in the paragraphs above, what would happen if you, say, in your first month of payments made your payment of $877.57, and ALSO sent in your next month's principal payment? That's right, if you guessed it. You'd never be paying the interest on that $44.61 from the second month of your loan onward. Right there, you would have saved $832.96 in total interest payments on your loan.

Now, how would this compound your savings over time if you were to consistently, or even haphazardly, make additional principal payments towards your loan balance. We saw some examples of that in the preceding chapter, where we made extra principal payments of $25, $50 and $100.

Doubling your principal payment systematically, month after month, one would actually cut your term just about in half, and the total interest payments on the loan itself as well. The same basic effect can be achieved whether one makes the current month's payment, and also sends in double that month's principal payment, (i.e. in month #1 send in $877.57, plus tax and escrow of course, and also send an additional $44.24 marked for principal only) or, better yet, by sending in the month's payment, plus the next month's principal payment. The results are basically the same, but the latter plan pays the loan off a little bit faster and makes it easier to keep track of your current balance as you go along.

As you can see from the table in Chapter 1-2 of this book, and as you can see on your own loan amortization sheet, if you have one, doubling up on your principal payment early in your loan would probably not be all that much of a strain. The principal payments during this period of time are only about $45.50 pr month in the first two years of the loan, and don't hit even $100/month until into year nine of the regular amortization. By doubling your principal payment you will hit roughly $100/month principal in year 5 of your payments. For some, it could get tough to keep up these doubled payments into the latter part of the loan. Just keep in mind that your greatest savings are always going to be in the early part of your loan, and that any little bit extra you can do WILL make a difference, and, in many cases, a substantial difference.

As your loan balance is decreasing faster, of course, you also have more equity in your home than you ordinarily would have. At the end of year two on a regular payment plan, you would have only about $1300 equity, as compared with over $2600 equity on a doubled principal plan. At the end of year fifteen, your loan balance ordinarily would be $81,665.29, with $18,334.71 in equity. By doubling your principal payments, your loan balance at the end of fifteen years and two months would be $0.00, and your equity would, of course, be the full value of your house or property.

Chapter 2-5
Doubling Your Principal
and Interest Payment

There is something that can be done and monitored yourself if you have the extra funds to do it. That is, seeing what your principal and interest payment is monthly and just doubling that amount, again, being sure to mark the extra payment "For Principal Only" when you send it in. So, if your P&I (principal and interest) payment monthly is $1,200, paying $2,400 monthly will cut your 30 year term down to a total of 7 years. Now, you might wonder what practical application this method really has, as the majority of folks seem to make their monthly payments and not have a lot of excess left over to double that amount.

Well, I have two answers to this. One is that, while that is true, there are those who may, occasionally or consistently, have sufficient funds floating at the end of the month to do this, and instead of investing it otherwise, might find after a little figuring that it behooves them to invest in the very thing they are living in. After all, the increased and accelerated equity after a few years of living in their house paid down in this fashion would far outweigh the return on almost any conventional type of investment I could think of. I'll show you a table on this.

Loan Amount: $100,000

Interest Rate: 10%

Monthly Payment: $1755.14 ($877.57 x 2)

Year	Payment	Interest	Principal	Balance
1	$21,061.68	$9,478.66	$11,583.02	$88,416.98
2	$21,061.68	$8,265.77	$12,795.91	$75,621.07
3	$21,061.68	$6,925.87	$14,135.81	$61,621.26
4	$21,061.68	$5,445.67	$15,616.01	$45,869.25
5	$21,061.68	$3,810.46	$17,251.22	$28,618.03
6	$21,061.68	$2,004.02	$19,057.66	$ 9,560.37
6.5	$21,061.68	$ 266.20	$ 9,560.37	0

This loan would be paid off in 6 years and 6 months, with total interest payments of $36,196.65.

Compare the standard payment schedule on this loan:

Loan Amount: $100,000

Interest Rate 10%

Monthly Payment: $877.57

Year	Payments	Interest	Principal	Balance
1	$10,530.84	$9,974.98	$ 555.86	$99,444.14
2	$10,530.84	$9,916.77	$ 614.07	$98,830.07
3	$10,530.84	$9,852.46	$ 678.38	$98,151.69
4	$10,530.84	$9,781.44	$ 749.40	$97,402.29
5	$10,530.84	$9,702.96	$ 827.88	$96,574.41
6	$10,530.84	$9,616.27	$ 914.57	$95,659.84
6.5	$10,530.84	$4,682.84	$ 408.77	$95,167.26

Instead of having paid off just under $5,000 of that loan in 6 years and 6 months, by doubling your principal and interest payment, that same loan would be paid in full, with full equity in the house.

Many may not be able to afford to pay their loan down in this way. A solution? Buy a smaller house. That may sound like a bad compromise, but look at it from a business standpoint. After two years of double payments in a $100,000 loan, there is almost $25,000 equity in the house. After three years, there is nearly $40,000 equity. In six years, it's close enough to being paid off to buy a house twice the size and not change your payments one bit. Add to that equity market increases and the value of your home really becomes the value of your home, because it's yours.

Chapter 2-6
Combining Solutions

I earlier promised you some good news on the 40-year loan. On a 40-year loan, I have seen dramatic savings in both interest and term using a combination of the various systems mentioned in this book.

I recall one couple who obtained a 40-year adjustable rate loan. They took this 40-year loan because they had a large loan amount and were offered zero points with a 40-year term. I expected some savings and a reduced term, but I did not expect the magnitude of what I found when I worked up their analysis for them. As one scenario offered them, they could have taken that $350,000 loan and, by going onto a bi-weekly system of mortgage reduction (see Chapter 2-2), and making fixed monthly payments of $3,000 principal and interest, they would have reduced their interest payments by over $500,000 and reduced their 40 year term to a little over 18.5 years. This was making payments only slightly higher than their bank was calling for, and it kept their monthly payments at a constant, with only the amount going towards interest changing monthly. Of course, this option was based on assumed interest activity, but the particular loan they chose kept the interest fluctuations relatively mild and predictable.

This analysis more than cut their 40 year-term in half and saved them over half a million dollars interest. Successes such as this can be easily achieved just by knowing and understanding the principles and theory behind present day mortgage loans, and by understanding and applying the principles in this book.

Chapter 2-7
Summary

As you can see, there are many, many things that can be done with a mortgage, with assistance from a mortgage consultant or a Bi-Weekly Mortgage Reduction Company, or without. Knowing the data in this book and whatever other information learned by trial and error, or just plain common sense, there is plenty one can do with their home mortgage to really succeed in the area of home ownership. Whether your interest is in dramatically reducing your total mortgage payments, decreasing your term or simply increasing your net worth, there is undoubtedly a mortgage reduction plan that is right for you.

My first intention with this book was to help the average home buyer to get informed about the facts behind his or her home mortgage loan, so as to vastly increase the possibility or likelihood of home ownership in the near future. I think for all your hard work and mortgage payments, you deserve that. If I have accomplished that in any small part, then I will consider the time spent in writing this book to have been worthwhile.

My second intention with this book was to point out that anything can be learned and understood. It just takes a little willingness to look, to break the thing down into its parts and to digest the information.

And for those who seem to make it a habit to try and make things appear difficult to understand, or be part of an elite, "in the know" group of individuals, well, may they get mired down in their own complexities in life and enjoy only the company of each other, doomed in that environment to not understand anything of what the other is saying.

So, good luck to you. I wish you well in all of your endeavors.

Glossary of Terms

Closing - The time in which the purchaser and seller meet with the settlement officer to sign all documents to effect sale of the property, (or transfer of the title to a new lender in the case of refinancing), secure a new mortgage and transfer monies related to the transaction. In the case of a refinancing situation, this would be the homeowner and a representative of the lender.

Closing Costs - Closing costs are the costs involved in purchasing a property or obtaining a loan.

Equity - The difference between the value of your home and the amount of mortgage or loans taken against it.

Escrow - Money held in trust by a third party until such time as the transaction between the initial two parties is completed.

Interest - Interest is money owed or paid for the use of borrowed money. It is also the rate of such payment expressed as a percentage over time.

Points - A point is an amount of money equal to 1% of the loan amount. It is service charge paid to the lender for giving a loan. The number of points which are charged varies depending on the interest rate being charged and other financial market conditions.

Prime Rate - This is the interest rate charged by a bank to its most credit worthy customers. It is also called Prime Interest Rate.

Principal - The principal is the outstanding balance due on the loan.

Principal & Interest (P&I) - Your principal and interest payment is the total of your principal payment and the interest amount paid at that time.

Settlement - Settlement is the time in which the purchaser and the seller (or the home owner and a representative of the lender) meet to sign all documents to effect sale of the property (or transfer of the title to a new lender in the case of refinancing), and to transfer all monies related to the transaction. See *Closing*.

Tax and Insurance Escrows - Your lender may require that they pay future property tax and fire insurance bills for you. If so, the lender will require that an escrow account be established at the time of settlement. The initial escrow amount can be obtained from your lender. The total of the property taxes and insurance sums for the year are divided into twelve equal installments and this amount is then added to your monthly principal and interest amount. This part of your total monthly payment, then, goes into this account and accrues until such time as these tax and insurance payments are due, at which time your lender pays them for you. Your lender has a vested interest in ensuring any property taxes and insurance payments are made and are made on time, as the failure to pay these in a timely manner can cause the property to be lost to the tax collection agency or to fire, flood or other damage. For this reason, the lender does not like to leave it to chance that every homeowner will pay these bills on time.

Your total monthly payment, then, generally consists of both your Principal & Interest payment as well as the tax and insurance escrow monies. If taxes go up, or insurance rates go up, your lender is notified and he, in turn, notifies you that your monthly payment will increase by 1/12 of that amount.

Index